I0540314

THIS BOOK BELONGS TO

_____

FOR THE KIDS WHO WANT TO WIN

ISBN: 9798894582580

IN THE HEART OF A SMALL VILLAGE, LIVED A YOUNG APPRENTICE NAMED AIDEN. HE WAS LEARNING THE ANCIENT ART OF SHADOW MAGIC UNDER MASTER VARO'S WATCHFUL EYE.

MASTER VARO WAS THE GREATEST SHADOW MAGE IN THE LAND, AND AIDEN WAS EXCITED TO BECOME JUST LIKE HIM. BUT THERE WAS ONE PROBLEM: AIDEN COULDN'T MAKE SHADOWS OBEY HIM.

EVERY TIME AIDEN TRIED TO SUMMON A SHADOW, IT WOULD EITHER FLOAT AWAY OR CURL
UP INTO AN UNRECOGNIZABLE SHAPE. "YOU MUST BELIEVE IN THE MAGIC WITHIN YOU,
" MASTER VARO WOULD SAY.

ONE CRISP EVENING, MASTER VARO LED AIDEN TO THE SHADOW GROVE, A MAGICAL FOREST WHERE SHADOWS WHISPERED SECRETS. "THIS IS WHERE YOU'LL LEARN," HE SAID. "SHADOWS ARE YOUR TEACHERS HERE."

AIDEN STARED AT THE SHADOWS STRETCHING ACROSS THE TREES. THEY SEEMED SO ALIVE. "HOW CAN I MAKE THEM LISTEN?" HE ASKED. MASTER VARO SMILED, HIS EYES TWINKLING.

"YOU MUST FIRST TRUST YOUR SHADOWS. THEY ARE NOT JUST DARK; THEY ARE FULL OF UNTOLD MAGIC. THEY NEED A GUIDE, SOMEONE WHO CAN SEE BEYOND THE DARKNESS."

AIDEN TOOK A DEEP BREATH AND STRETCHED OUT HIS HAND. A SMALL SHADOW
FLICKERED ON THE GROUND. IT DIDN'T MOVE. "YOU'RE NOT TRYING
HARD ENOUGH," WHISPERED MASTER VARO.

AIDEN CLOSED HIS EYES AND IMAGINED THE SHADOWS DANCING, MOVING WITH GRACE.
HE OPENED THEM AGAIN. THE SHADOW WOBBLED, BUT IT STAYED CLOSE.
A SMALL SMILE TUGGED AT AIDEN'S LIPS.

THE NEXT DAY, AIDEN PRACTICED AGAIN. HE WAVED HIS HAND, TRYING TO BEND A SHADOW, BUT IT SLIPPED AWAY LIKE WATER THROUGH HIS FINGERS. HIS HEART SANK. IT WAS HARDER THAN HE THOUGHT.

"I JUST CAN'T DO IT," AIDEN SIGHED, SITTING DOWN ON A STONE. MASTER VARO
APPEARED BESIDE HIM, HIS VOICE GENTLE. "YOU NEED PATIENCE.
THE SHADOWS WILL COME WHEN YOU ARE READY."

LATER THAT NIGHT, AIDEN WANDERED THE VILLAGE, HIS MIND RACING. SHADOWS SWIRLED AROUND HIM, BUT NONE OF THEM SEEMED TO LISTEN. THEN, HE NOTICED SOMETHING STRANGE—A SHADOW FOLLOWING HIM.

AT FIRST, AIDEN THOUGHT IT WAS HIS IMAGINATION, BUT THE SHADOW SWAYED IN TIME WITH HIS STEPS. HE STOPPED, AND THE SHADOW STOPPED. "I'M NOT ALONE," AIDEN THOUGHT, FEELING A SPARK OF HOPE.

THE NEXT MORNING, MASTER VARO LED AIDEN DEEPER INTO THE SHADOW GROVE.
THE TREES HERE WERE ANCIENT, THEIR TRUNKS WRAPPED IN DARK VINES.
SHADOWS FLICKERED LIKE LIVING CREATURES.

"TO CONTROL SHADOWS, YOU MUST FIRST LEARN TO SEE THEIR TRUE NATURE,
" MASTER VARO EXPLAINED. "THEY ARE NOT JUST DARKNESS;
THEY ARE REFLECTIONS OF THE WORLD AROUND US."

AIDEN STARED AT THE SHADOWS AROUND HIM. SOME WERE LONG AND STRETCHING, WHILE OTHERS WERE TINY AND STILL. "HOW DO I MAKE THEM DO WHAT I WANT?" AIDEN ASKED.

"SHADOWS LISTEN TO THOSE WHO ARE PATIENT AND KIND. THEY WILL REVEAL THEIR SECRETS TO YOU WHEN YOU TRUST THEM," MASTER VARO SAID. AIDEN NODDED, DETERMINED TO TRY AGAIN.

AIDEN CLOSED HIS EYES AND THOUGHT OF THE SHADOWS AS FRIENDS, NOT THINGS TO CONTROL. SLOWLY, HE LIFTED HIS HAND. THE SHADOW BESIDE HIM TWITCHED. HE SMILED. IT WAS A START.

THAT EVENING, AIDEN RETURNED TO THE GROVE. THE SHADOWS FELT DIFFERENT TONIGHT,
AS THOUGH THEY WERE WAITING FOR HIM. HE RAISED HIS HANDS AND FOCUSED,
GENTLY PULLING THE SHADOW CLOSER.

THIS TIME, THE SHADOW OBEYED. IT CURLED AROUND HIS FEET, GROWING AND SHRINKING
WITH HIS MOVEMENTS. AIDEN GASPED. HE HAD DONE IT!
THE SHADOWS WERE STARTING TO LISTEN!

BUT AS THE SHADOWS BEGAN TO DANCE, A LOUD RUSTLE SOUNDED FROM THE TREES.
SUDDENLY, A DARK FIGURE EMERGED FROM THE SHADOWS. IT WAS A CREATURE,
TALL AND MADE OF SWIRLING DARKNESS.

"WHO DARES DISTURB MY FOREST?" THE CREATURE GROWLED, ITS VOICE DEEP AND COLD.
AIDEN STEPPED BACK, FEAR CREEPING INTO HIS CHEST. MASTER VARO
STOOD TALL, HIS EYES STEADY.

"DO NOT BE AFRAID, AIDEN," MASTER VARO SAID CALMLY. "THIS IS A SHADOW BEAST, A GUARDIAN OF THE GROVE. TO PASS, YOU MUST SHOW THAT YOU TRULY UNDERSTAND THE MAGIC OF SHADOWS."

THE SHADOW BEAST CIRCLED THEM, ITS GLOWING EYES PIERCING THE DARK. AIDEN'S
HEART RACED. HE COULD FEEL THE POWER OF THE SHADOWS AROUND HIM.
"I MUST TRY," AIDEN WHISPERED TO HIMSELF.

WITH A DEEP BREATH, AIDEN RAISED HIS HAND. SHADOWS SWIRLED AROUND HIM, FORMING
A PROTECTIVE SHIELD. THE CREATURE GROWLED BUT COULDN'T BREAK THROUGH.
AIDEN HAD FINALLY FOUND HIS STRENGTH.

THE SHADOW BEAST STEPPED BACK, NODDING ITS HEAD. "YOU HAVE LEARNED WELL, YOUNG ONE. YOU UNDERSTAND THE TRUE POWER OF SHADOWS. YOU MAY PASS."

MASTER VARO SMILED. "YOU HAVE DONE IT, AIDEN. YOU TRUSTED THE SHADOWS, AND THEY TRUSTED YOU IN RETURN." AIDEN BEAMED, HIS HEART SWELLING WITH PRIDE.

AS THEY CONTINUED DEEPER INTO THE GROVE, AIDEN REALIZED THAT SHADOWS WEREN'T JUST TOOLS TO BE USED. THEY WERE ALIVE, FULL OF MAGIC, WAITING TO REVEAL THEIR SECRETS TO THOSE WHO TRULY UNDERSTOOD.

BY THE END OF THE WEEK, AIDEN HAD LEARNED TO BEND SHADOWS TO HIS WILL.
HE COULD MAKE THEM STRETCH, TWIST, AND EVEN DANCE LIKE FLAMES.
BUT THE SHADOWS HAD BECOME MORE THAN MAGIC.

THEY HAD BECOME HIS COMPANIONS. EACH SHADOW TAUGHT HIM A LESSON—PATIENCE, KINDNESS, AND TRUST. AIDEN KNEW HE STILL HAD MUCH TO LEARN, BUT HE WAS READY FOR THE JOURNEY AHEAD.

ONE DAY, AS THEY WALKED THROUGH THE FOREST, MASTER VARO LOOKED AT AIDEN
WITH PRIDE. "YOU ARE READY TO BEGIN YOUR OWN PATH. THE SHADOWS
WILL ALWAYS BE WITH YOU."

AIDEN SMILED, LOOKING AT HIS SHADOW, NOW FAMILIAR AND COMFORTING. HE KNEW THAT WHEREVER HE WENT, THE SHADOWS WOULD BE THERE TO GUIDE HIM, JUST AS THEY HAD ALWAYS BEEN.

AIDEN RETURNED TO THE VILLAGE, HIS HEART LIGHT. AS HE PASSED THROUGH THE
STREETS, HE NOTICED THE SHADOWS AROUND HIM—THE WAY THEY FLICKERED
IN THE SUNLIGHT, STRETCHING AND SHIFTING.

HE REACHED OUT TO THE NEAREST SHADOW, AND THIS TIME, IT DIDN'T HESITATE.
IT CURLED AROUND HIS HAND LIKE AN OLD FRIEND, AND AIDEN LAUGHED IN JOY.

AIDEN KNEW THAT THERE WOULD BE CHALLENGES AHEAD, BUT NOW, WITH THE MAGIC OF
SHADOWS AT HIS SIDE, HE WAS READY TO FACE WHATEVER CAME HIS WAY.

"GOODBYE FOR NOW, SHADOWS," AIDEN WHISPERED, LOOKING BACK AT THE FOREST. "I WILL BE BACK SOON." AND WITH THAT, AIDEN SET OFF, THE SHADOWS DANCING BESIDE HIM.

MASTER VARO WATCHED FROM THE FOREST EDGE. HE KNEW HIS APPRENTICE HAD
LEARNED ALL HE NEEDED TO KNOW. AIDEN'S JOURNEY WAS JUST BEGINNING.

AS THE SUN SET, CASTING LONG SHADOWS ACROSS THE LAND, AIDEN'S SHADOW STRETCHED OUT BEFORE HIM, READY TO LEAD HIM ON NEW ADVENTURES.

AIDEN WALKED PROUDLY, KNOWING THAT NO MATTER WHERE HE WENT, THE MAGIC OF
THE SHADOWS WOULD ALWAYS BE THERE, WAITING FOR HIM TO
UNCOVER ITS MYSTERIES.

AND SO, THE YOUNG SHADOW MAGE'S JOURNEY BEGAN, FILLED WITH NEW FRIENDS,
NEW DISCOVERIES, AND THE PROMISE THAT SHADOWS WOULD ALWAYS HOLD
THEIR MAGIC—IF YOU KNEW HOW TO SEE IT.

THE END... OR IS IT JUST THE BEGINNING?

www.ingramcontent.com/pod-product-compliance
Lightning Source LLC
Chambersburg PA
CBHW081541120626
46550CB00009B/2820